Original title:

The Frosted Hourglass

Copyright © 2024 Creative Arts Management OÜ
All rights reserved.

Author: Nolan Kingsley
ISBN HARDBACK: 978-9916-94-486-8
ISBN PAPERBACK: 978-9916-94-487-5

The Quiet Sands of Winter

When snowflakes dance and giggle low,
The winter wind whispers, "Oh, go slow!"
A snowman sighs, 'Is this my year?
I forgot how to smile; please bring me cheer!'

Brrr, the ground is colder than my jokes,
Even the rabbits wear scarves like folks!
They hop and slide as if on a spree,
While I just stumble repeatedly.

Snowflakes in the Hourglass

Time slips away like melting ice,
Each flake that falls has its own vice.
As it lands, it whispers, 'Hey, look here!
I'll crack a joke before I disappear!'

I see my cocoa dance with delight,
Swirling in foam, what a funny sight!
Yet every hot sip feels like a dare,
Will it jump from my mug? Oh, don't you care?

Whims of Frost and Memory

Memories freeze like popsicles bright,
Each one a tale, oh what a delight!
Frosted giggles echo the past,
As I reminisce, but not too fast.

The flowers in winter wear coats so bold,
While sun-kissed memories gather dust untold.
The trees rustle gossip, make no debate,
About last year's snowman—was he first-rate?

Crystal Corners of Time

In crystal corners where giggles reign,
Time has a habit of being quite vain.
It loves to slow down during ducky slides,
While my hat's lost, tangled by its rides.

Each minute swaggers, full of its glee,
Pretending it rules, oh can't you see?
But as frosty moments begin to slip,
I chased a squirrel—oh, what a trip!

A Tapestry of Chill

In the corner sits a cat,
Wearing mittens, think of that!
Chasing snowflakes with delight,
Oh, the joy of winter's bite!

Frosted flakes on my hot tea,
Laughter dances, wild and free.
Sipping cocoa, slipping on ice,
Winter's antics sound quite nice!

Socks are lost, they're on the roof,
Snowmen hold the best of proof.
With each slide and every fall,
We freeze our giggles, oh so small!

When the sun breaks through the gray,
Sunburnt noses steal the day.
Cards and games on frozen ground,
Winter's joy, forever found!

Hushed Hours in Winter's Glass

Rumors whisper through the snow,
A bear's dance? No one could know!
Fluffy boots and hats askew,
Winter giggles just for you.

Snowballs fly like a wild dream,
Laughter bursts; we sing and scream.
Teeth chattering with frostbite grins,
Playing tag while the snow begins.

Hot cider in my frozen hands,
I pretend to make snowman bands.
Twirling in the chilly air,
Hilarity, everywhere!

As bedtime creeps, in snuggy beds,
Visions of snow fights fill our heads.
In the night, a snow globe spins,
Dreaming of our winter wins!

Drifted Memories of a Frozen Journey

A slips and slides parade begins,
Watch the penguins have their spins!
Snowflake hats that start to melt,
Warm and fuzzy, how we've felt.

Scarf's too long, it holds a joke,
Entangled feet, a dashing stroke.
Catching snowballs on the chin,
Laughter echoes, winter's win!

Echoing laughs beneath the trees,
Falling stars? Nope, just a sneeze!
Gliding past on frozen lakes,
A symphony of happy flakes.

When the sun starts warming days,
We'll applaud our silly plays.
Memories swirled in frosty air,
Creating tales that we all share!

Freezing Shadows of Time

Once there lived a jolly fool,
Built a snowman, lost his drool.
Monkey suits in shades of white,
Skiing down the driveway fright.

Snowy whispers painting the night,
Chasing shadows, what a sight!
Lollipops adorned with frost,
In this game, we can't be lost!

Hot soup bubbling, steam afloat,
Chilly noses, lend a coat!
Running wild with frozen glee,
Time stands still, or so it seems!

When warmth returns, oh what a scene,
Snowmen down, just like a dream.
Memories made, we'll crack a grin,
Longing for that chill again!

When Sand Meets Snow

In winter's chill, the sand does freeze,
It dances 'round like playful bees.
With every grain, a snowball flies,
As laughter soars and time just sighs.

The clock does giggle, tick-tock, tick-tock,
While snowflakes melt on cuckoo's clock.
Who needs a beach when you have this?
Just grab a shovel, you won't miss!

The Icy Grip of Time

Time slips away, or so they say,
But in the frost, it loves to play.
A frosty hand that gives a shove,
With a wink and nudge, oh how it does love!

Every minute shivers in the breeze,
While ice cream cones bob up with ease.
"Chill out!" they scream, as they melt too fast,
In this frozen game, the fun will last!

Glimmering Frost and Shadow

A sparkly dance in the dusky light,
Where snowmen giggle with pure delight.
Under moonlit skies, they sway and glide,
In a frosty world where fun can't hide.

Frosty friends with hats so tall,
They hold a party, come one, come all!
With carrot noses and scarves so bright,
You'll laugh and sing through the snowy night!

In the Silence of Frost

In the hush of snow, the world stands still,
But snowflakes tumble with endless thrill.
   Each flake a jester, spinning in glee,
   Whispering secrets for you and me.

   With a twitchy nose and frosty toes,
   We tumble and slide, oh how it flows!
   A swirling dance, what fate we find,
   In the icy silence, we're all entwined.

Shimmering Hourglass of Solitude

Tick-tock, the sand's a prankster,
It jumps and skips like a dancer.
Pour it out and watch it glow,
Who knew hours could put on a show?

In solitude, the grains collide,
They giggle softly, there's no need to hide.
A frosty grin upon the face,
Time's just a jester in a funny place.

Memories Frozen at Dawn

With a snap, the memories freeze,
Captured like jokes in a box with ease.
Each moment a snowflake, unique and bright,
Laughter lingers, oh what a sight!

At dawn, they twirl in the crisp cold air,
Whispering giggles without a care.
They dance past clocks, no need to stall,
Frozen in laughter, enchanting us all.

Seasons Behind a Glass Veil

Behind the veil, the seasons play,
Winter slips into a summer ballet.
Springs are splashed with autumn's cheer,
Time's just a puppet in a funny sphere.

The glass may fog, but watch them tease,
Shaking up leaves like a wild breeze.
They chuckle and poke at the ticking time,
In this funny world, everything's a rhyme.

Transience in Frosted Grain

Grains are laughing; they know the trick,
Slipping through fingers, oh so slick.
Frosty hugs at every turn,
Time's a comedian, always to learn.

Frozen moments want to play,
Twist and shout, they've got quite a display.
Reality cracks in a whimsical jolt,
In this frosted kingdom, humor's our vault.

Reflections in a Chilled Vessel

Inside this glass, time does jiggle,
As ice cubes clink and quietly giggle.
Moments slide, like butter on toast,
Time seems to play the silliest ghost.

The seconds dance, in a comic spree,
Like socks on a dog, they're wild and free.
Every tick-tock wears a funny hat,
Waiting for lunch or a quick chit-chat.

Laughter bubbles in a frozen bowl,
While seconds frolic, making us whole.
Time takes a break, to smell the stew,
In this frosty flight, we laugh anew.

Pour another glass; let's raise a cheer,
For frozen laughs that keep drawing near.
Each sip a giggle, a belly-filled jest,
In the chilled vessel, we find our rest.

Moments Frozen in Crystal Clarity

Time froze in a glassy delight,
Like a snowman trying to take flight.
Each moment trapped in a riddle so bright,
A shiny spectacle, pure comedy sight.

Tick-tock, tickle, the seconds unwind,
Like a rubber chicken left far behind.
In every sparkle, a giggle resides,
Glimmers of humor where silence collides.

Dancing with glee, the minutes cascade,
As we point and laugh at the silly charade.
Each dollop of time, a unique little prank,
Wishing the clock would join in the tank.

So raise your glass, let the laughter grow,
In frozen fun, we let good times glow.
These moments encased in a crystal shroud,
Brings haberdashers a giggle-proud crowd.

The Silent Dance of Hourglass Winds

Winds whisper tales in the frosty air,
As time pirouettes, without a care.
Sand on the move, with no steps to guide,
An hourglass party, where all can glide.

Tickles from seconds float past like dust,
Moments ensconced in absurdity's trust.
The dance is silly, the music is free,
Even the shadows join in for a spree.

A flicker of fun as the sands take a spin,
A duet of giggles drenched in the din.
Time frolics and tumbles, a jester's delight,
While we clap our hands in a puzzling flight.

So let's sidestep worries and dance all night,
Embracing the wind's whimsical flight.
In the stillness of time's playful tease,
We find sweet laughter, our hearts to appease.

Frost-Kissed Memories of the Past

Frosted moments, all wrapped in cheer,
Tickled by memories that dance near.
The past like a snowball, round and bright,
Hurls itself back in a whimsical flight.

Each laugh crystallized in frosty frames,
Replays the times when we played silly games.
Polar bear antics and giggles so stout,
In every frosted picture, joy leaps out.

Recalling those days when we fell on ice,
Slip-sliding doo-dah, oh what a slice!
The memories chuckle, a playful revolt,
Spinning us back to a giggle-filled jolt.

So gather the stories that frost cannot thaw,
In a chilly embrace, we find the awe.
Each frosty whisper, each tickle of time,
Turns memories sweet into giggles that rhyme.

Time's Wintery Embrace

Tick-tock said the frosty clock,
Clearly stuck at half-past shock.
Time wears mittens, oh so thick,
Wrapped in scarves, a chilly trick.

Snowflakes dance with every tick,
As hours melt like ice-cube slick.
Laughing at the clock's delight,
Wishing for a summer night.

But wait! Who's the real sly one,
Telling jokes while time does run?
In winter's grip, we laugh and play,
Counting laughs 'til it's someday!

Oh frosty friend, you jest and poke,
Chasing moments like a cloak!
While time slips by in winter's waltz,
The cold itself is full of faults!

Fleeting Moments in the Chill

Each second struts in frosty pants,
Doing crazy winter dances.
With every tick my socks do slide,
On icy floors, a silly ride!

Frozen laughter fills the air,
While snowmen plot without a care.
Can we steal a moment or two,
Before the chill bids us adieu?

Juggling snowballs, oh what fun!
Time's a jester, on the run.
Count the seconds with a grin,
As we frolic, our cheeks all thin!

Grab your hat and hold it tight,
Time is sneaky in the night.
With every giggle, winter gleams,
As moments slip like melted dreams!

Echoing through the Frost

In this winter's freezing fight,
Time echoes back in pure delight.
With frosty whispers all around,
Moments giggle, lost, then found.

Icicles hang like words unsaid,
As seconds skitter, filled with dread.
Yet laughter warms this icy plight,
A merry chase through day and night.

Snowballs thrown, a jesters game,
With chilly antics, none to blame.
Time's a prankster, bold and brash,
A winter wonder, quick and rash!

So gather 'round, let's share some cheer,
For icy moments bring us near.
We'll dance through frost, make the best,
In laughter's arms, we find our rest!

Captivity of the Icy Flow

In the realm where cold winds blow,
Time's a captive, moving slow.
Caught in webs of winter's thread,
With shivery thoughts and visions spread.

Rolling snowballs, sleds in tow,
Chasing time, where did it go?
Frosty fun, a ticklish game,
While minutes melt like candle flame.

A snowflake's wink, a twinkle bright,
Taunts us as we hold on tight.
Can you catch a second or two,
Before it disappears from view?

So here we laugh, while days are fraught,
In this frosted dance, our time is caught.
With shivery glee, we make it shine,
In icy moments, we intertwine!

Drifts of Time in Crystal Clarity

In a land where seconds slip away,
Chocolate candies melt and sway.
The clocks all giggle, what a sight,
As ice cream sundaes take to flight.

Ticky-tock, the minutes tease,
Frosty giggles in the breeze.
A snowman cracking jokes galore,
He says, "I'm busy, ice cream's on the floor!"

The hours drape in snowy cheer,
Whipped cream clouds are gathering near.
Spoons entwined in a playful war,
Each scoop's a laugh we'll all adore.

While whiskers frost on noses bright,
The sledding hills become our light.
In each drifty tick we find the fun,
Time's a joke, we're never done!

Seasons Drifting in Icy Whispers

Snowflakes dance with silly flair,
Whispers tickle through the air.
Winter winks with frosty glee,
As squirrels slide on frosty brie.

In the winter sun, we play with time,
Joking with icicles, oh so prime.
The calendar laughs at a snowman's cap,
He's wearing boots, oh, what a flap!

As spring rolls in, we chase the thaw,
Time tickles us; we dance in awe.
With raindrops giggling on our nose,
This merry chase, the laughter grows.

Seasons swirl in snow globe schemes,
Sipping cocoa, laughing at dreams.
In the frost, life's a merry spin,
Time, oh time, let the fun begin!

Forever in a Frozen Echo

Echoes bounce in frosty halls,
Laughter brightens winter's calls.
An ice cube juggles, what a sight,
Tickling clocks with every bite.

Puddles chuckle, splashes play,
Hours march in a comical way.
Bouncing snowballs, a playful fight,
Chasing shadows into the night.

Each tick is wrapped in winter's grin,
Time's a snowman wearing thin.
With each soft crunch beneath our feet,
We carve the joy; it's quite the feat.

Forever stuck in giggles bright,
In frozen frames, we find our light.
The echoes yawn, they all can see,
Time's funny bone, it's so carefree!

Time's Frosted Canvas

Painting moments, icy gleam,
Time splashes colors, what a dream.
Frosty brushes, giggly strokes,
Snowman artists, full of jokes.

With every layer, laughter swirls,
As time twirls like nuts in curls.
Glittering hours slip through our hands,
We craft our fun on winter's sands.

In a gallery of frozen cheer,
Clocks waltz in sync, winter's near.
Each tick a brush, each tock a flurry,
Artful moments in a lovely hurry.

So take a seat, sip cocoa's steam,
Life's a canvas, so let's beam.
In frosted fun, we surely thrive,
Where time's a joke—we're so alive!

Grains of Snow

In winter's grip, the shovels dance,
As flakes fall down, they take their chance.
A snowman sighs, it looks so round,
He chills with every joke we've found.

A snowball fight, so expertly planned,
But wind turns aim into a bland.
With laughter bright and cheeks aglow,
We cheer the grains of frozen snow.

Hot cocoa brews, a sweet delight,
But spills abound, what a frosty sight!
The marshmallows float, they tease and play,
As winter smiles, it's just our way.

Through icy paths, we slip and slide,
With mittened hands, we laugh and glide.
Each frosty breath, a cloud so slow,
In winter's fun, we swiftly flow.

Remnants of a Frozen Dawn

At dawn's soft break, the world is white,
A frozen scene, a pure delight.
But as the sun begins to shine,
Those snowy trails become divine.

Socks and boots in mismatched pairs,
Tugging along, oh the chilly glares!
The remnants tease, they slowly melt,
With every drip, more warmth is felt.

A cup of tea, steam rises high,
While snowmen watch with a wistful sigh.
Their carrot noses in dismay,
As winter bids a funny sway.

So here we are, with laughs to spare,
A frozen dawn that's light as air.
These remnants gleam, they come and go,
In giggles soft, we steal the show.

On the Edge of Ice and Time

On winter's edge, the snowflakes fall,
They laugh and tumble, a snowy brawl.
With ice beneath our hesitant feet,
We teeter on the edge of sweet.

With every slip, we shriek and cheer,
The frosty fun, it draws us near.
From tumbles loud to giggling sighs,
We dance and play beneath the skies.

While sleds take flight on hills of white,
We race and spin with sheer delight.
But oops! There goes another glove,
As time stands still, we laugh and shove.

The season spins, it twirls so fast,
On ice and time, we grasp that blast.
With winter's tricks and playful glee,
We ride the waves, just you and me.

Whirlwinds of Frost and Grain

A flurry swirls, so wild and free,
It tickles noses, glee-filled spree.
With frosted breath that dances bright,
We whirl in grains of pure delight.

The baker giggles, flour in hand,
Counting the snowflakes that touch the land.
His cookies roast, a warm embrace,
As frosty friends we share our space.

The wind howls jokes that twist and spin,
Each frozen whim leads us to grin.
With giggles light, we chase the cold,
In whirls of fun, our hearts unfold.

So gather round, let's spin and sway,
In frosty grains we'll laugh and play.
With every chuckle, winter's spun,
In frosty fun, we're all but one.

Slumbering Seconds Beneath the Ice

Time's playing hide and seek, oh dear,
The clock is stuck, it's quite unclear.
Seconds dance with frozen glee,
While I sip tea, just let it be.

I saw a minute trip and fall,
Wrapped in a scarf, it's not so tall.
Laughing at hours, oh what a sight,
They slipped on ice, quite a delight!

The moments snooze in chilly air,
Napping away without a care.
Comfy seconds with frosted grins,
Playing games, oh where to begin?

So let them lounge, these lazy ticks,
As I enjoy my frozen mix.
With every tick, a chuckle flows,
In this land where time just doze.

The Glint of Memory in Frosted Glass

There's a sparkle in the mist, oh gosh,
Memories swirl like whipped up posh.
Reflections giggle, dance, and play,
In the glass, where thoughts drift away.

I thought I saw my last ice cream,
Winking back, like in a dream.
Scoops of laughter in frozen frames,
Each taste a silly game of names.

Moments jostle in a funny brawl,
Catching snowflakes, bouncing them all.
Tickled by the echoes of cheer,
Time takes a selfie, grinning ear to ear.

With every sip from this chilled cup,
Memories rise, never back up.
I raise a toast to frosty fun,
In glassy glint, the laughter's spun.

Snowflakes on the Edge of Time

Snowflakes tumble with a wink,
Teasing time, don't you think?
They land, then giggle, float away,
On the edge, they love to play.

Each flake has tales of silly deeds,
Carving paths, as fun proceeds.
Chasing moments with silly grace,
What a hop, what a race!

Tick-tock pauses for a laugh,
While snowmen plot a wacky gaffe.
They gather round with frosty cheer,
Making winter parties here!

So let the snowflakes tumble down,
And wrap the world in a frosty gown.
In laughter's freeze, we spin and rhyme,
On this edge, we chase the time.

The Winter's Silence of Passages Past

In the stillness where silence roams,
Time's like a snowman without homes.
Muffled giggles on frosty nights,
Whispers echo, oh what delights!

Each second takes a snowy leap,
Waddling to dreams, all snug and deep.
With jackets thick and scarves askew,
They tumble down, just for a view.

Frosted whispers tell old tales,
Of trips and slips on icy trails.
Winter's humor, grand and sly,
As moments mingle, giggle, and fly.

So grab a mitt and join the fun,
In the chill where laughter spun.
For even silence wears a grin,
In the dance of where we've been.

When Time Stands Still in Winter's Veil

In winter's chill, the clocks amiss,
A penguin laughs, does a little twist.
Snowflakes dance, but time won't flow,
My socks are warm, but the cold winds blow.

Tea brewed strong, it spills on me,
A frosty cat climbs up a tree.
The minutes slide, they laugh and play,
While I search for my lost scone tray.

Ice cream melts, but not my grin,
As winter's games, they just begin.
Jokes on me, try to keep up,
Don't forget, I still have my cup!

Caught in a snow globe, what a sight,
Even snowmen join the festive fight.
Laughs echo through the frosty night,
With winter's charm, it's pure delight.

Fables of a Frozen Continuum

Once in a land of frozen tales,
Waddling ducks wear tiny trails.
A snowman sneezed, and off he flew,
With a carrot stick, he bid adieu.

Time froze fast, or so it seems,
Caught in a loop of chilly dreams.
Icicles giggle, hang in the sun,
They shatter with laughter, oh what fun!

Fables told of socks in pairs,
Mittens lost in snowball layers.
The clock's hands twirl, like winter's breath,
Chasing snowflakes, a dance with death.

Laughter rings through winter's delight,
As penguins skate in silly flight.
Oh frozen day, you jest and play,
How I wish you'd just melt away!

Timeless Echoes in an Icy Embrace

An echo's giggle through snowy trees,
Time's a prankster, it bends with ease.
Frosty whispers, frozen light,
Countdown to dinner, but it's all a bite.

Popsicles glow in the winter night,
While roasted chestnuts warm the light.
Sirens call from the frosted glen,
"Join us for fun in the chilly den!"

A toaster burns toast; what a smell!
In winter's grip, who can tell?
Rabbits hop through a powdered quest,
While icicles hang, they jest and jest.

Timeless moments, they tickle your soul,
Tick tock sings, but it won't console.
Embracing the frost in laughter's spree,
Come share the giggles, come share with me!

The Chill of Vanished Days

Days like snowflakes, they flutter and fade,
Laughing hearts in the frozen parade.
Hot chocolate spills, oh what a fuss,
A marshmallow splat, just made a plus!

Chill in the air, but I wear a grin,
Snowmen strategize to toss in a win.
Sledding down hills, oh what a thrill,
As time stands still, we climb back up hill.

Voices echo through shivering air,
Where winter's leprechauns hide with care.
They chuckle and cheer, a snowman's ball,
A cascade of laughter, the best gift of all.

Yet with each giggle, time loses its grip,
Like hot cocoa spills on an ice-cold trip.
So toast to the chill, for all it brings,
In the fair freeze of life, let laughter sing!

Shards of a Frozen Echo

In a land where time stands still,
Icicles dance, what a thrill!
Tick-tock sounds like a snowplow,
Time is lost, don't ask me how.

The sand is icy, not so neat,
Frosty clocks and chilly feet.
I tried to brew my tea just right,
But ended up with a snowball fight.

Each grain of time does slip and slide,
Like a penguin on a winter ride.
I shed a tear, but then I grin,
For frosty fun will always win!

In the corner sits a frozen grin,
Laughing hard, where do I begin?
With every slip, a chuckle rings,
In a frostbit world, we dance on springs.

Frosted Memories in Grain

The clock's hands freeze on every hour,
Snowflakes dance, they hold the power.
With each tick, a giggle peeks,
In a world where frosty fun speaks.

Sand gets cold, what a surprise,
Time and chill, in sweet disguise.
I filled a cup with slushy notes,
Time for tea? It surely gloats!

My watch is dusted, all aglow,
In the frigid air, we steal the show.
With jests that linger like ice cream,
In frozen lands, we drift and dream.

Grains of time, they shiver by,
Like snowmen who just learned to fly.
So let's embrace this icy cheer,
For frosted joys bring us near!

Frozen Minutes, Melted Dreams

Minutes trickle like melting ice,
In the winter's heart, oh so nice.
I tried to race against the clock,
But ended up in a snowman's flock.

Each second laughs, a jolly tease,
Tickled by the chilly breeze.
Fumbles and tumbles, we all see,
Life's a joke—just wait and freeze!

In the pause, we slip and slide,
Memories drift, what a wild ride!
Every moment wrapped in frost,
Chasing laughter, never lost.

We dance like snowflakes in delight,
Chasing time till the stars ignite.
With dreams that melt in puddles of cheer,
Here's to laughter, bright and clear!

Captured in Crystal

In a bottle forged of icy dreams,
Time looks through in sparkly beams.
I wrote my wishes on the frost,
Now everything feels like a playful cost.

Every second's a crystal ball,
Where giggles freeze and snowflakes sprawl.
I stepped outside, my hair turned white,
Frolicking in the snowy light.

Each grain of sand, a frosty race,
Yet I can't keep a serious face.
Caught in laughter, it's plain to see,
Time's a jester, come laugh with me!

Captured moments, a playful tease,
A life full of fun, if you please.
In a world where chuckles never cease,
We find joy in the frosted lease.

Moments in an Icebound Realm

In a realm of ice, so cold and bright,
Snowmen giggle at the frosty sight.
Penguins wearing scarves, what a delight,
Skating on the pond, oh what a fright!

Chilly winds whisper, tickling our ears,
While snowflakes dance, igniting our cheers.
Hot cocoa brews, calming our fears,
In this wintry world, laughter appears.

Bunnies hop by in their fuzzy best,
Building snow forts, they never get rest.
With frosty whiskers, they put us to test,
In a snowball fight, we're clearly possessed!

So raise your mugs, let happiness flow,
In this icebound realm, let chuckles grow.
With every freeze, and every warm glow,
Time ticks in laughter, like endless snow.

Temporal Frost

In a world where minutes freeze and gleam,
Come take a ride on the icy stream.
With frozen clocks, we're stuck in a dream,
Wandering through time, hear the frosty theme.

Snowflakes tumble, wishing for a break,
While winter squirrels plot their grand mistake.
Building tiny castles, oh for goodness' sake!
In this chilly kingdom, we're all wide awake!

A turkey in mittens, what a sight to see,
Chasing after snowballs, oh so carefree.
Nature's odd humor, just let it be,
Laughing with frost on our hot cup of tea.

So dance with the frost, twirl in the air,
Time may be frozen, but laughter's laid bare.
In the whimsical waltz, we have none to spare,
Just giggles and grins in the brisk winter care.

Hourglass of Winter's Breath

Snowdrifts collect in a comical heap,
While toppled sleds cause a giggling sweep.
A snowball thrown, a secret to keep,
As frosty wind whispers, 'Don't make me peep!'

Icicles dangle, like teeth out of place,
In this chilly race, we quicken our pace.
With muffled laughter, we cover our face,
Winter's a prankster, setting the pace.

Time slips like ice, under our feet,
Each tick is a snowflake, soft and sweet.
Running through snow, what a delightful feat,
In this merry madness, frosty and neat!

So grab your mittens, join in the cheer,
In this frozen moment, there's naught to fear.
With each frosty breath, let joy reappear,
As seasons change, our laughter endear!

Nature's Frigid Timekeeper

Nature's clock ticks in a snowy ballet,
With pine trees dressed for a winter soiree.
Hats on the snowmen, let's frolic and play,
While chirpy birds squawk, 'Is spring on the way?'

Frosted branches wave, a humorous sight,
As squirrels gather nuts, all day and night.
A dance on the snow, everything feels right,
In this frozen land, everything's light!

Hot soup in a mug, steamy and bright,
Tickles our noses, warms us outright.
As penguins slide past, oh what a flight,
Laughter erupts in the frosty twilight.

So cherish the moments where winter does thrive,
In the heart of the cold, we feel so alive.
With smiles everlasting, oh how we thrive,
In nature's embrace, we joyfully jive!

Chronicles Beneath a Glassy Veil

Under a dome of chilly spark,
The sand dances like a playful lark.
Time's tickle is a silly game,
We laugh as it forgets our name.

Once it slipped, that sneaky grain,
Chased by giggles, oh what a pain!
It rolled away, what a surprise,
A runaway in disguise!

Worms in mittens, snowflakes tease,
They tumble around, like breeze in trees.
Every moment, a prankster's delight,
Even shadows skip in frosty light.

A wink from the clock, with a cheeky grin,
Each tick a jest, let the fun begin!
In this realm of glimmer and gleam,
Time's a jester, or so it seems.

Silhouettes of Time in a Snowbound Case

In winter's grip, we brave the chill,
Snowflakes fall with giggles that thrill.
The shadows dance, the clocks converse,
Time's silly side is a frosty curse.

Hiccups in seconds, hiccups in laughs,
Moments slipping, like greasy halves.
All in a case, the fun won't cease,
Twirling seconds, spinning with ease.

Giggles echo, can you feel the burn?
As seconds flip, it's time for a turn.
Frost coats the laughter, thick and white,
In this zany realm of frosty delight.

A snowman sneezes, the hourglass grins,
Clocks don scarves; oh where do we begin?
In this whimsied world of frosted praise,
Each tick is a jest, in a frosty haze.

A Minute's Breath in Frost's Grasp

A minute's breath, a cheeky breeze,
Frosty whispers tease the trees.
Time snickers at the antics near,
Slipping on ice, we cheer and cheer.

The calories of laughter burn bright,
As snowflakes giggle and take flight.
Every moment a comic spun,
Grin wide, for we're not yet done!

Ticks and tocks in playful chase,
A merry dance, oh what a race!
In icy depths, we share a laugh,
Time's a goof, a bubbly gaff.

So let's toast to this chilly spree,
With frosted drinks, a jamboree!
Each second's tick is a joke to find,
In frozen laughter, we unwind.

Echoes from the Frozen Abyss

From the depths of icy realms, we sigh,
Where time stretches, truth does lie.
Tickling echoes in frosty air,
Laughter bubbles, a playful affair.

In this abyss, the seconds yawn,
Towards horizons, the giggles are drawn.
Snowflakes tease like whispers low,
Echoes bounce in a frosty flow.

With each chilly wobble, we shake,
Moments teasing like a snowflake.
Frosty jokes in winter's hold,
A laughter treasure, worth more than gold.

While time may freeze, humor won't cease,
In this paradise, we find our peace.
So hail the giggles, let them soar,
In the frozen realms, we laugh some more.

Visions Rendered in Icebound Grain

In a world where time's a slippery thief,
Grains of laughter tumble, oh what a relief!
The clock ticks backward, a funny old trick,
As I slip on ice, hoping not to get sick.

Frozen moments dance in a jigsaw parade,
Chasing my thoughts like a playful cascade.
I trip on a memory, who put that there?
And chuckle at moments, light as the air.

A snowman grins wide with a starfish cackle,
While frozen toes wiggle in a chilly tackle.
Time melts like butter on a sunny toast,
As I laugh with the seconds, I love the most.

So here's to time, with its quirks and its brawls,
It's a slippery dance through the frosty ball.
May we chuckle and grin as the moments collide,
In the whimsical wonder of winter's glide.

The Lament of Stilled Sands

Sands of time have taken a nap,
A snooze so deep, it lost its map.
Tick-tock, where did the minutes go?
Oh look, there's a snowman wearing a bow!

The hourglass sits with a twinkling frown,
Sands stuck together like they were in a gown.
Time's frozen feast at the winter's fair,
Grab a spoon, folks, time's a creamy layer!

With ketchup on ice and cookies that freeze,
We giggle and snort with frosty unease.
A timer for laughter, oh what a jest,
In this jolly game, we're all truly blessed.

So here's to stilled sands, a spirited crowd,
With giggles and jokes, we dance out loud.
Let's toast to the moments we can barely see,
As we fill up our glasses with glee and frosty tea!

Enigma of the Icy Cycle

Round and round like a merry-go-round,
Time slips and slides without making a sound.
It likes to play tricks, oh what a tease,
As I search for my glasses stuck under some cheese!

Frosted faces laugh with a wink of a smile,
As seconds freeze like a woolly old style.
The calendar giggles, it's hard to believe,
That winter can be both a trickster and thief.

I tried to catch time on a sledding spree,
But fell on my bum, oh what a sight to see!
Now I'm stuck in a cycle of frosty delight,
As icicles hang on the edge of the night.

So let's dance in circles, around snowy dreams,
With giggles and chuckles, we twist and beam.
In this icy enigma, we're lost but so found,
As we weave through the laughter in snow-covered ground.

Yearning Through Frosted Echoes

Echoes of giggles bounce like a ball,
In the frosted air, we're having a ball.
Each tick of the clock brings a chilly delight,
As we slide like penguins through laughter at night.

Wishing on snowflakes that jingle with cheer,
We giggle at shadows that wiggle near.
A dance on the ice with whipped cream and sprinkles,
As frosty whispers tickle and crinkle!

Yearning for laughter in layers so thick,
While snowflakes tease with their crystalline trick.
The echoes repeat like a joke gone awry,
Yet here in the cold, we still laugh and sigh.

So let's embrace the frost with a comfortable sigh,
In this funny adventure where time's always sly.
With each frosted echo, let's celebrate play,
And fill up our hours in the silliest way!

Crystalline Countdown

In the kitchen, ice wine spills,
While grandma attempts her skills.
The cake she made, a frozen treat,
With sprinkles that refuse to eat.

The clock is ticking, oh, so slow,
Time's a prankster, don't you know?
The bubbly pops, the glasses clink,
While we debate the time to drink.

Watch the clock, it gives a grin,
As we sparkle and begin.
The timer laughs, oh what a show,
It seems so keen to steal the dough.

Yet here we dance with snowflakes bright,
Mistakes are made, but all feels right.
When last year's cookies go awry,
We giggle hard, oh me, oh my!

Silhouettes in the Snow

Snowmen dance with floppy hats,
Chasing squirrels and furry cats.
Their carrot noses, firm and cold,
Flop down, leaving stories bold.

The sun peeks out with little glee,
"Who's stealing my rays?" cries he.
Snow boots got stuck in snowy pits,
"Help!" cries one through frosty fits.

The ice melts down, what a fright!
Raindrops fall, but feels just right.
Laugh lines form, oh what a jest,
Like snowflakes in the winter dressed.

While snowflakes giggle on the ground,
We're silly, spinning all around.
In winter fun, our hearts aglow,
Time flickers by, oh do take it slow!

Sculpted by Time's Grip

The sculptor's chisel finds a whim,
Creating statues, tall and slim.
Each year they pose in frozen grace,
But no one sees their funny face.

Tick-tock giggles fill the air,
As snowmen start to comb their hair.
With frosty breaths, they chat and jest,
"Am I the tallest? I'm the best!"

A snowball flies, it lands, oh dear!
"Watch out!" The frosty friends all cheer.
With shouts and laughter, mayhem reigns,
As winter plays its silly games.

And when the sculptures start to sway,
They wink at us and fade away.
Oh, mirthful time, be kind and spry,
Sculpted moments, don't let them fly!

The Dance of Frost and Time

The moonlight sparkles, winter's gleam,
As frosty figures twist and dream.
On icy floors, they start to sway,
"Oh look! I've lost my hat today!"

The ice skates glide in silly spins,
While laughter flows as fun begins.
The snowballs fly like tiny ships,
As cold on cheeks turns to comic quips.

A slippery dance, oh what a sight!
With every fall, we take flight.
Time laughs and cracks a frosty smile,
Contagious joy stretched mile by mile.

Frosty whispers in the air,
"Don't be shy, come join my flair!"
The clock won't stop, but that's okay,
For fun lasts longer than the day!

Winter's Silent Countdown

In winter's chill, time seems to freeze,
Snowflakes dance, like silly bees.
Icicles dangle, like frozen jokes,
Tick-tock's lost in snowman's pokes.

Socks on the line, they wave goodbye,
While snowmen giggle, oh me, oh my!
The clock's lost track, in holiday spree,
Who needs a watch? Not you and me!

Mittens missing, they play hide and seek,
While jolly old frost takes a little peek.
Chattering teeth do a comic act,
In winter's embrace, we stay intact!

So raise a mug, let laughter ring,
In snowy fun, we find our spring.
As snowmen melt, the chaos will brew,
Time isn't real; it's what we construe!

Fragments of a Frozen Past

Old photos stuck in a snowy frame,
Laughing at winter, what a strange game!
The past slips by like a sled on ice,
Each moment captured, but not too nice.

Grandpa's mittens, a mismatched pair,
He wears them proudly, without a care.
Hot cocoa spills, a marshmallow fight,
Frozen in memory, a sweet delight!

Snowball battles, a comically missed shot,
We're all so clumsy, but who cares a lot?
With every slip, comes a dorky cheer,
Fragments of fun that keeps reappearing near!

Let's toast to mishaps, and moments we keep,
In a season of laughter, not losing sleep.
In frozen fragments, hilarity reigns,
As we dance through the cold, holding our reins!

Frost-Kissed Sand and Shadows

In winter's glow, oops, there goes the sun,
Frost-kissed shadows play, oh what fun!
Sandmen building in a snow-clad beach,
With floppy hats, they try to teach.

Sandy snowballs, a chilly delight,
Flying through the air, oh what a sight!
While penguins jog, in tiny warm gear,
They waddle and giggle, never show fear.

Beneath fluffy clouds, where snowflakes reign,
We chase after shadows, so hard to explain.
A frozen sandcastle, a twist on the norm,
In this frosty world, we weather the storm!

So gather your friends, and let laughter soar,
In frosty sands, we always want more.
Each chilly moment, a giggling spree,
In the heart of winter, just you and me!

Glacial Reflections

A mirror of ice shows the silliness near,
Where faces contort, and laughter we hear.
Snowflakes are hats on our heads so high,
In glacial reflections, we giggle and sigh.

Frosty companions, all dressed up snug,
We twirl through the flakes, like a big happy bug.
With snowman guides, we wander around,
Finding silly treasures on wintery ground.

In this frozen fun, we spin and we glide,
Sharing our stories, with friends by our side.
Laughing at temps that make noses red,
In glacial mirrors, no worries to dread.

As puns may freeze in the chilly air,
We'll warm up our hearts, with love and flair.
So come take a peek, at the laughter we sow,
In glacial reflections, let the warmth grow!

Captured in Ice

Time tick-tocks in frozen frames,
Silly moments, oh what games!
Sand so cold, it starts to gleam,
Catching giggles, what a dream!

Tickle the grains, watch them slide,
Frosty laughs, we can't abide!
Watch us chuckle, as we race,
In our boots, we slip with grace!

Ice cream cones, but oh so chill,
Licking snowflakes, what a thrill!
Each grain holds a frosty tale,
In a world that's set to sail!

Giggling sands in frosty hues,
Stories shared, the flurry ensues.
Life in frost, a merry show,
Dance on ice, let laughter flow!

Echoes Through the Chill

In this land of icy giggles,
Frozen whispers, playful wiggles.
Froze in time, oh what a trap,
Echoes bouncing, a hilarious map!

Snowflakes twirl, a quirky ballet,
Friends dressed warm in bright display.
Old man winter's jokes so dry,
He cracks us up, we sigh and cry!

Sand slips past, a comical race,
Chasing moments, we quicken pace.
Frosty fables in the breeze,
Laughs resounding, oh such tease!

Each tick tock gives a hearty cheer,
Frosty chuckles, oh my dear!
Through the chill, we find our way,
In the freeze, we laugh and play!

Frosted Mementos

Memories frozen, what a sight,
Laughter wrapped up, tight and bright.
Grains of giggles in chilly clumps,
Replaying joy in frosted lumps!

Time behaves like slippery soap,
Slipping past with goofy hope.
Sledding down the icy slopes,
Giggles echo—our heart's elopes!

Frozen antics in every grain,
Winter's fun is never mundane!
Snowball fights and frosty cheers,
Tickling moments through the years!

Snapshots filled with chilly grace,
In our hearts, they find their place.
With each chuckle, we weave the tale,
Laughing into the winter gale!

The Chill of Passing Seasons

Seasons change, but laughter stays,
Chilling moments in funny ways.
Snowmen with hats that flop and slide,
In winter's grasp, we take a ride!

Sand trickles down with a playful cheer,
Snowflakes fall, but joy stays near.
Frosty breezes, tickle and tease,
Moments frozen in a frozen freeze!

Each tick is but a shivery jest,
As we bundle up, in scarves, we're dressed.
A giggle today, tomorrow a roar,
Winter's grin, we can't ignore!

Ice-cold chuckles line the way,
Frosty frolics on display.
In the chill, we find our song,
Captured laughter, where we belong!

Paradox of Icy Winds

Once I thought I'd warm my toes,
But ice just said, 'Oh, take a dose!'
Now socks and shoes are lost in time,
But boy, those chilling winds do rhyme.

With every gust, a laugh appears,
I trip in snow, while sipping beers.
The slippery path is life's new dance,
My frozen jig—a frosty prance.

Who knew that winter had such flair?
It throws a party, unaware.
Each flake that falls, a joker's game,
In frosty fun, I find my fame.

So here's to sun that rarely beams,
And snowflakes caught in silly dreams.
I wear my scarf like a goofy crown,
In frosty fashion, I'll strut around.

Embrace of Cold and Memory

A chilly hug from winter's ghost,
Cold air that tickles, I love it most.
Frosty fingers wake the past,
In every belly laugh, a chill holds fast.

Memories swirl like snowflakes bright,
Each one a story, each one a bite.
I slip on ice, but I'm still keen
To share tales of my frozen sheen.

Laughter echoes in the crackling frost,
As I declare, 'I'll never be lost!'
With every tumble, a grin on my face,
Winter's embrace is a slapstick grace.

So bring on the blizzards, hail, and sleet,
I'll dance through the cold with frosty feet.
In a world where ice becomes my friend,
Every chilly moment, I'm sure to extend.

Whispers of Time Encased in Ice

Time tick-tocks with frigid breaths,
Each chime of frost, it jokes and hefts.
Icicles jingle as minutes slide,
In this frosty hour, joy and pride.

I found a penguin, or was it a duck?
Either way, we share some luck.
Sliding around on glossy sheets,
Laughing at time, oh how it cheats!

Every second trapped in glimmering freeze,
While I sip cocoa with giggles and wheeze.
The clock just giggles; I give it a wink,
Dear frosty moments, let's not overthink!

So here's to tickles in the chilly air,
And frosty whispers without a care.
In the ice-encased world, we gleefully play,
With time's jolly spirit, forever we stay.

Sands of Winter's Embrace

The sand is frozen, what a sight!
I thought I'd sunbathe, but it's a fright.
Frosty grains make castles of ice,
In this winter beach, it's all quite nice.

Sleds replace boards on the snowy shore,
As chilly winds invite us to explore.
We toss snowballs like grains in a dune,
While laughing at the frost beneath the moon.

Every flake falls like a grain in time,
Creating laughter like a quirky rhyme.
Cold waves crash with a chilly cheer,
In this frosty wonderland, let's persevere!

So bring out the mittens, let's take a ride,
With snow-people smiling, we won't hide.
In winter's embrace, let the fun unfurl,
As we build a castle in this frozen world.

The Silent Toll of Winter

When snowflakes dance with silly grace,
The world transforms, a white embrace.
Yet time stands still, it takes a break,
As squirrels plot mischief for goodness' sake.

Tick-tock, I say, the clock is slow,
As frostbite tickles, just like a show.
The winter sun, a shy little friend,
Can't decide if it wants to stay or bend.

With mittens on, I wave to the trees,
Who chuckle back, rustling in the breeze.
The winter coat feels heavy and loud,
While snowmen wink, gathering a crowd.

So here we are, in chilly delight,
With giggles trapped in the frosty night.
The clock may tick with snickers and jests,
As winter giggles in comical quests.

Icebound Dreams and Moments

An ice cream dream in arctic air,
With penguins sliding without a care.
I thought of summer, sunny and bright,
But here comes winter, not quite polite.

Moments freeze in silly poses,
While frost-bitten noses become our roses.
A snowball fight erupts with delight,
Mystic laughter, oh what a sight!

Icicles hang, like teeth so white,
While penguins prance, oh what a fright!
Ice-bound dreams, oh what a tease,
Fumbling around like it's a breeze.

The moments tick while snowflakes dive,
Reminding us just how to thrive.
A funny waltz in the world of freeze,
Where every giggle finds ways to please.

Fading Light in Frosted Glass

The sun peeks in, a sly little sprite,
Through frosty glass with a timid bite.
Shadows play games, hide and seek,
As winter whispers, 'Come out, don't freak!'

Rays tickle noses, oh what a date,
While trees wear coats and laugh at fate.
A piglet slips on a patch of ice,
Squealing loudly, 'Now that's not nice!'

The fading light dances and sways,
A comical end to winter's long days.
With every chuckle, the laughter grows,
While color dances in chilly prose.

So smile through the fog of winter's embrace,
With each moment, there's joy to chase.
For in the frosted glass, we find,
A hilarious world, gently entwined.

Crystalized Footprints in Time

Footprints twinkle like diamonds on ice,
As snowflakes giggle, oh so nice!
Every step, a funky dance,
In a world where winter takes a chance.

The squirrels chime in with a quirky song,
As if to say, 'You can't go wrong!'
The playful cold wraps around our feet,
While laughter echoes down every street.

Winter grins with frost on its cheek,
Teasing our toes, it's far from meek.
We chase the snowflakes like little kids,
Making memories with each joy that bids.

So step with gusto, take on the chill,
For every moment brings laughter and thrill.
Crystalized footprints, a treasure we find,
In this funny winter, our hearts are aligned.

The Glacial Memento Mori

In the garden of twilight, a snail takes a stroll,
Wearing boots made of ice, with a glimmering soul.
Tick-tock goes the clock, but it's frozen in place,
As time trips on snowflakes, trying to keep pace.

A penguin in a tux, tiptoes through the chill,
Juggling winter snowballs, a comedic thrill.
"Watch out!" cries the squirrel, "He's coming in hot!"
But he slips on a patch, and forgets what he's got.

Beneath frosty banners, old ghosts start to laugh,
As snowmen discuss their next biblical gaffe.
"Did you hear?" said one with a carrot for a nose,
"That time really freezes, in a land full of prose!"

So raise a cold toast, to the moments gone wild,
In the icy grip of humor, we remain like a child.
With each crystal chuckle, we count down the fun,
While time lets out giggles, but never will run.

Time's Breath in the Winter's Grip

An hourglass hangs from a dead winter's tree,
Where seconds wear mittens, and time likes to pee.
The mice in their jackets are sneaking about,
While snowflakes are dancing, without any doubt.

A chicken with popcorn is waiting for space,
To join in the frolic, the grand winter race.
As sand slips through fingers, it quacks "What a show!"
While the hours keep egging the minutes to slow.

The clock strikes a winter, with a grand old chime,
Rabbits in top hats, oh, how they do rhyme!
"We dine here at dusk, for a banquet of snickers,
And marshmallow fluff served with hot cocoa flickers!"

In this frosty enclosure, where laughter ignites,
The punchlines are chilled, but the joy's out of sight.
With each slippery second, we bubble and glide,
For in winter's embrace, we all get to slide!

Shadows of Eternity in Hallowed Frost

Within shadows that giggle, there's laughter at dawn,
The stars play hopscotch on the frost-covered lawn.
Ghosts sharing jokes with a snow-laden oak,
As the wispy winds whisper their best funny poke.

A polar bear wonders, "What's this human craze?
Dancing in circles to shake off the glaze?"
But time's frozen piñata begs kids for a hit,
And each swing brings giggles as snow sparks and flits.

The sundial is snoring while clocks learn to snicker,
The owls roll their eyes—oh, the hours are quicker!
Then winter wraps blankets around grinning stars,
As the universe snorts at its own silly scars.

So cherish the moments that come with a wink,
As shadows of laughter in frost start to shrink.
For time may be silly, in this frostbitten glow,
But the joy of the present is all that we know.

Rime's Tapestry of Lost Hours

In the weave of the rime, antics begin,
As time trips over itself in a march with a grin.
The chandeliers glimmer, frozen high in the air,
With snowflakes like confetti, waving without care.

Slips and slides on the wisdom of thawing ice beds,
As a snowman named Bob spins tales in his threads.
"Hey, watch me take flight," he declares with a cheer,
And promptly falls over, rolling with no fear.

"The calendar's a prankster," crows a cheeky crow,
"Who's counting the seconds when the laughter won't slow?"
Amidst winter's petunias, the chill tickles the toes,
While giggles spread wider than anyone knows.

So dance in the frost, let your humor run free,
As time takes a tumble beneath the old tree.
In this tapestry of rime, may we never forget,
That laughter's the secret, we'll never regret!

Sand and Ice: A Delicate Dance

In a world where sand meets frost,
The grains are laughing, no matter the cost.
They dance on whims, in a silly race,
With icy slips and sandy grace.

The clock's all dizzy, having a fit,
Mixing up time, oh what a hit!
Silly seconds just can't agree,
Tickling each other, oh such folly!

The sun throws shade, while the frost winks,
As if they're plotting, or so one thinks.
Catch a falling star, pull it in tight,
But it turns to steam, oh what a sight!

Though time may tumble with frosty flair,
Silly moments are beyond compare.
So laugh, dear friend, as the minutes slide,
In this comical whirl, let joy be your guide.

Ethereal Frost

Frosty whispers on the window pane,
Giggling softly, driving us insane.
Time's a jester, with a wobbly grin,
Just tickled pink by the chaos within.

Snowflakes tumble, each one a prank,
On a frozen pond, they did a prank tank.
They slide and spin, with a flip and a flop,
Wishing they'd never decided to stop.

Each second teeters, on the edge of fun,
Like frosty cupcakes ready to run.
The joy is sweet, like candy and cream,
In this silly dance, we all laugh and beam.

With icicles swinging from tree to tree,
Every moment's a joke, can you see?
So raise a toast, to the icy cheer,
In this frosty giggle, we'll have no fear.

Temporal Glaciers

Glaciers prance in a silly parade,
Each one wearing a hat, a frosty charade.
They mold and they shift, with a shiver and shake,
Creating a laugh at the dawn's first wake.

Time takes a trip on a sled made of ice,
Sliding down hills, oh isn't that nice?
Giggles erupt from the chill in the air,
As everyone slips, without a care.

Seconds freeze-frame, in a playful light,
Spinning like tops, what a glorious sight!
The clock's having fun, what a silly feat,
Pushing us all toward a jiggly beat.

So cherish the moments, let laughter prevail,
In this whirling dance, we'll never grow pale.
For life is a joke, so come join the rhyme,
As we frolic and play in this whimsical time.

Wintry Sands of Time

Sands of winter, a funny old sight,
Tickling the toes, as day greets night.
Every grain giggles as it starts to fall,
Like a snowball fight, oh let's have a brawl!

Time takes a tumble, headed for bliss,
Frosty confetti in a cheerful twist.
It dances and twirls, singing a tune,
One minute chilly, the next one in June.

The clocks are melting, like ice cream cones,
With a splat and a giggle, the laughter drones.
Sandcastles jest where icicles hang,
Plotting a coup—Oh what a prank!

So gather around, for this frosty spree,
With laughter and joy, wild and free.
In this playful wormhole, let us unwind,
For the silliest moments are the best kind.

Chilled Moments and Icy Grains

In a clock made of snow, the minutes take flight,
Sipping hot cocoa while avoiding the blight.
Time slips on ice, a slippery show,
As I chase after seconds that dance in the snow.

A penguin in slippers slips past with a wink,
Counting the hours with frost on the brink.
The toast of old time, now frozen and cool,
Where once was a fountain now flows a cold pool.

We're scaling the moments, it's quite the tall task,
To find a warm second, oh, do you dare ask?
But laughter's our sunshine, we wear it like crowns,
In this chilly charade, there are no frowns.

A snowman in shades haphazardly grins,
As we mash up the minutes, with all of our sins.
These frosty delights are a whimsical race,
In our frosted cocoon, there's humor and grace.

Translucent Time

Tick-tock in a snow globe, all fuzzy and bright,
As seconds go swirling in crystalline flight.
The past is translucent, it giggles and sways,
    Dancing in circles, in a frosty ballet.

A calendar's grinning, its pages all freeze,
With paper cuts healed by the chill of the breeze.
Each date is a snowflake, all different forms,
    Muffling the chaos of life's little storms.

We pop frozen bubbles, they burst with a laugh,
In this ice-cold merriment, we find our own path.
Ghosts of the minutes now play hide and seek,
    While time trips on ice with a comical squeak.

Dressed up as snowmen, we prance with delight,
Sharing tales of our winters that spark life's warm light.
In the realm of the frosted, we giggle and glow,
    Challenging time while we build in the snow.

Flickers of Frost

Watch as the seconds, like fireflies, twirl,
Wrapped up in scarves and a frosty swirl.
Each tick is a giggle, each tock is a tease,
Time's frozen laughter whispers through trees.

The calendar's breezy, it's slipping my mind,
Days melting like ice cream, one of a kind.
A comical rattling of hours in flight,
As I chase silly shadows that giggle with light.

Frosty-faced figures, they waddle and dance,
With a wink and a grin, they invite us to prance.
Their frosted confetti is sprinkled with cheer,
Turning chilling moments into laughter we hear.

With hot cocoa hats, we march, we glide,
In this world of frosted, we wear jokes with pride.
The clock's lost its rhythm, but who cares, it's fun,
In a flicker of frosty, we find we're all one.

Whispered Echoes of the Past

Echoes of laughter drift through icy walls,
Time tiptoeing softly while winter enthralls.
Footprints of giggles, now frozen in place,
Whispered secrets of time in this frosty space.

A snowball brigade! Oh, they trample and race,
With giggles and shivers, they hoot in the chase.
The clocks are all tangled in sheets of white fluff,
While moments of joy say, 'Hey, that's enough!'

With frosted mustaches, we laugh at the past,
Where minutes turn silly and run oh so fast.
The echoes bounce back from this whimsical time,
In a playful concerto, they dance and they rhyme.

So gather your friends in this season of cheer,
Let the echoes remind us that fun is quite near.
As winters hold whispers of magical light,
We savor each moment, a frosted delight.

Whispers of Icy Sands

In a land where snowflakes dance,
I found a clock that likes to prance.
It ticks in rhythm, oh so funny,
With hands that spin like dizzy honey.

The sands are frozen, stuck in place,
They giggle softly, never a race.
Time's a jester, pulls a mask,
Silly shadows in a frosty flask.

Each grain of snow, a playful sprite,
Hiding from the day, embracing the night.
They whisper secrets of winter's glee,
As I sip cocoa, under ice trees.

So here I stand in this snowy land,
With time like a snowman built by hand.
Laughing at moments that slip and slide,
In a world where snowmen often abide.

Time's Crystal Mirage

Through glassy realms of icy cheer,
I spy a clock that never steers.
With hands like mittens, fuzzy and bright,
It twirls and swirls in the frosty light.

It tickles time with a playful poke,
A whirling dervish, oh what a joke!
Seconds giggle, minutes blush,
As I race around in a silly rush.

Mirages of moments, blurry and sweet,
Slip from my grasp like a frosty treat.
Time freezes for giggles, slips on a peel,
Waltzing with laughter, that's the real deal.

So here we are, in this glimmering tale,
Chasing moments like a frosty snail.
With chuckles and grins, we dance in delight,
In a world where time is light as a kite.

Echoes in a Glass Oasis

In a glassy haven where giggles bloom,
Time hops around like a dancing broom.
Echoes resonating with laughter and cheer,
Moments tumble like snowflakes, so dear.

Frosted whispers wrap around,
Tickling ears with a merry sound.
Each second marches in silly shoes,
Wearing pajamas, sipping on brews.

Oasis of joy and frozen delight,
Time's a clown in this frosty sight.
It juggles hours like soft marshmallows,
Creating sweet chaos with soft mellow.

So join the fun in this icy dance,
Where moments frolic, leap, and prance.
Time's a friend who knows how to play,
In a world where laughter rules the day.

Chilling Embrace of Moments

In a world of laughter, snowflakes whirl,
Time gives a wink, as moments unfurl.
Each tick is a giggle, a tap of the toe,
As chilly hugs wrap around nice and slow.

Frozen in joy, we bounce and we sway,
Time plays the joker in a grand ballet.
Seconds slip by, like ice cream in sun,
Melted with laughter, oh what fun!

Tick-tock tickles and moments so bright,
Dancing with shadows in the pale moonlight.
Time's icy embrace is warm like a tease,
Filling our hearts with joy and with ease.

So let's grab those moments, frolic and play,
In this chilling laughter, we'll forever stay.
With smiles so big and hearts so free,
In a world where time's a whimsical spree.